What's it like to be a...
DENTIST

Written by Judith Stamper
Illustrated by Dana Gustafson

Troll Associates

Special Consultant: Dr. S. Stephen Keller, *Paramus, New Jersey.*

Library of Congress Cataloging-in-Publication Data

What's it like to be a dentist / by Judith Stamper; illustrated
by Dana Gustafson.
  p.   cm.—(Young careers)
  Summary: Describes the work done by a dentist as she examines,
cleans, and X-rays a patient's teeth.
  ISBN 0-8167-1799-0 (lib. bdg.)   ISBN 0-8167-1800-8 (pbk.)
  1. Dentistry—Vocational guidance—Juvenile literature.
[1. Dentists.   2. Occupations.]   I. Gustafson, Dana, ill.
II. Title.
RK60.S65   1990
617.6 '023—dc20   89-34392

What's it like to be a...
DENTIST

Dr. Amy Bennet walks into her examining room. A young boy is sitting in the dental chair. He has a white bib around his neck and a big frown on his face.

The dentist picks up the patient's record card. His name is Robby Sherman.

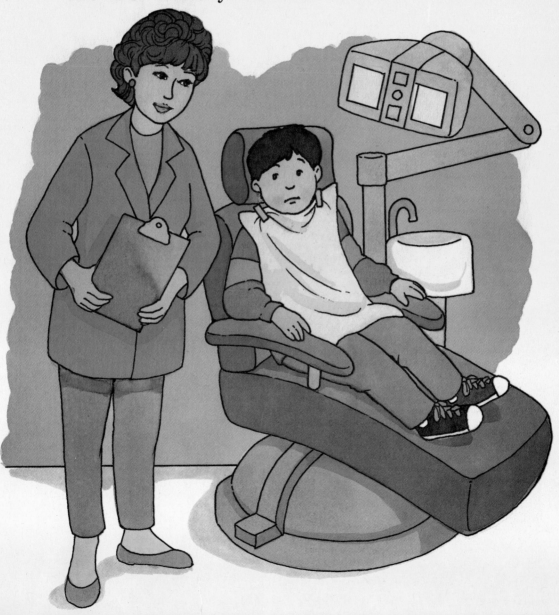

"Hello, Robby," she says. "This is your first visit to me, isn't it?"

Robby doesn't say a word. He just nods his head up and down.

"Are you afraid to open your mouth?" Dr. Bennet asks with a smile.

Robby nods his head again.

"I'll have to make you feel comfortable then," she says. "Did you know you're sitting in a special chair? It goes up and down. And it goes backwards and forwards."

The dentist presses levers at the bottom of the chair to make it move. Robby enjoys his ride. He even smiles and shows his teeth.

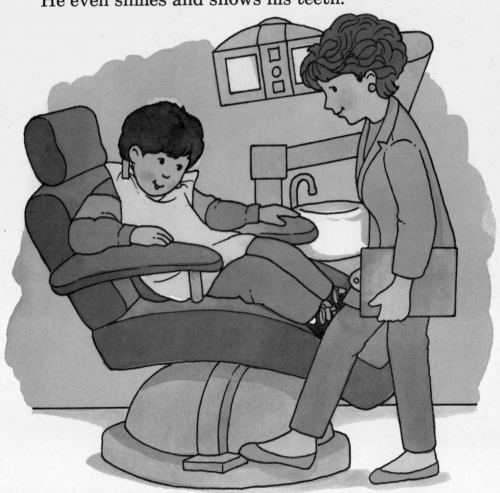

"This is my dental unit," Dr. Bennet goes on. "It holds the instruments I need to check your teeth."

The dentist takes an instrument from the small table on the unit.

"I use this mirror to look inside your mouth," she explains. "That big lamp gives me plenty of light." Dr. Bennet swings the overhead lamp into place. Robby squints at the light.

"Open up for a minute, Robby."

Slowly, Robby opens his mouth.

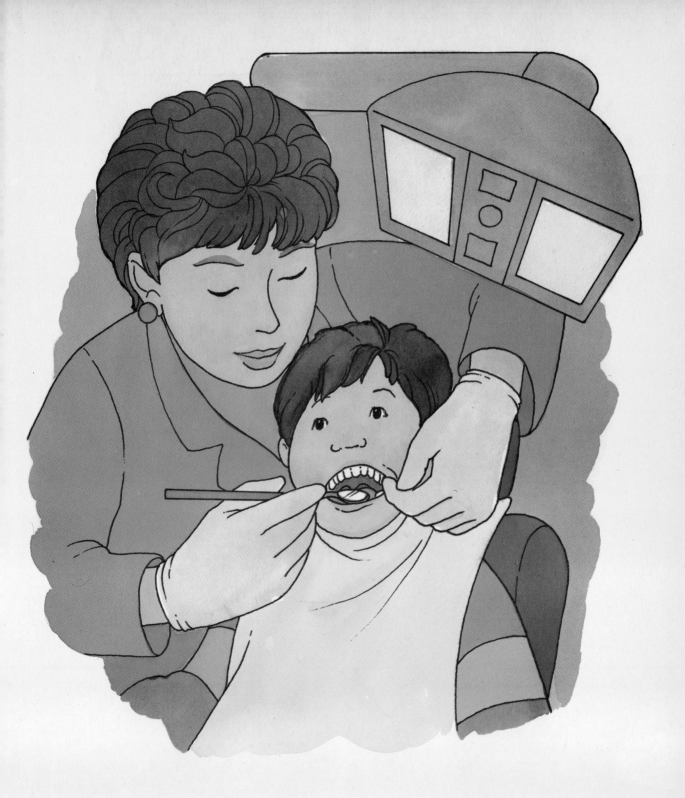

"This tool is called an explorer," Dr. Bennet says. She shows Robby a metal stick with a small point at the end.

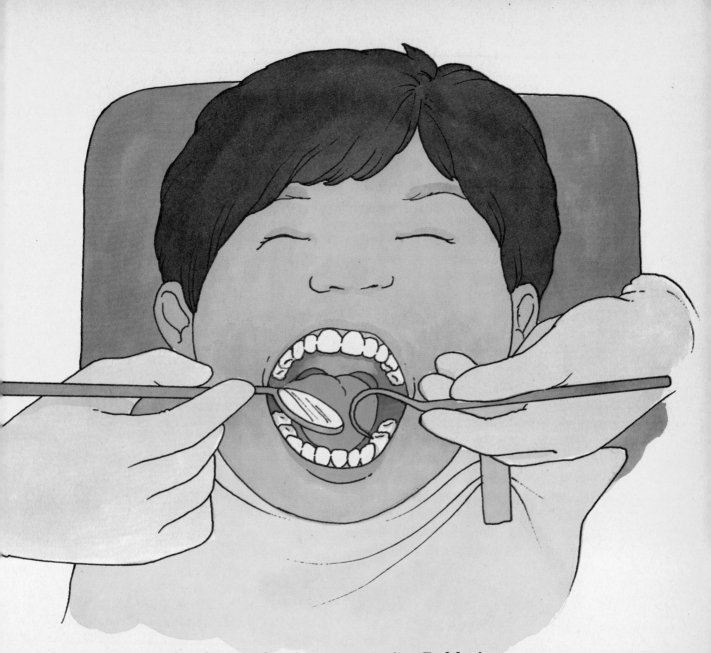

The dentist begins to examine Robby's
mouth. She presses the explorer against each
tooth.

"Very good, Robby. Now I'll clean your
teeth," Dr. Bennet says.

"First, I'm going to remove the tartar and plaque from your teeth," the dentist explains. "Tartar builds up like a crust. It usually forms between your teeth and in places that are hard to clean. Plaque can make your teeth decay. So I scrape both away with this." She picks up a scaler from the instrument table. It is curved at the end.

Robby squeezes his eyes shut. The scaler looks scary. But it doesn't hurt.

"Now, rinse," Dr. Bennet tells her patient. She presses down on a faucet on the dental unit. It fills a paper cup with water.

Robby takes a big sip of water. Dr. Bennet tells him to spit it into the rinse bowl.

"Next, I'll polish your teeth," the dentist says. "I use my drill for that."

Dr. Bennet picks up the handpiece of a long arm sticking out of the dental unit. She puts a rubber brush, called a buffer, on the end of the drill. Then she dips the brush into a special toothpaste.

"Open wide," the dentist says.

Robby opens his mouth again. Dr. Bennet starts the dental engine. The small brush tickles as it moves against Robby's teeth. Robby tries not to giggle. Soon, each tooth is polished and clean.

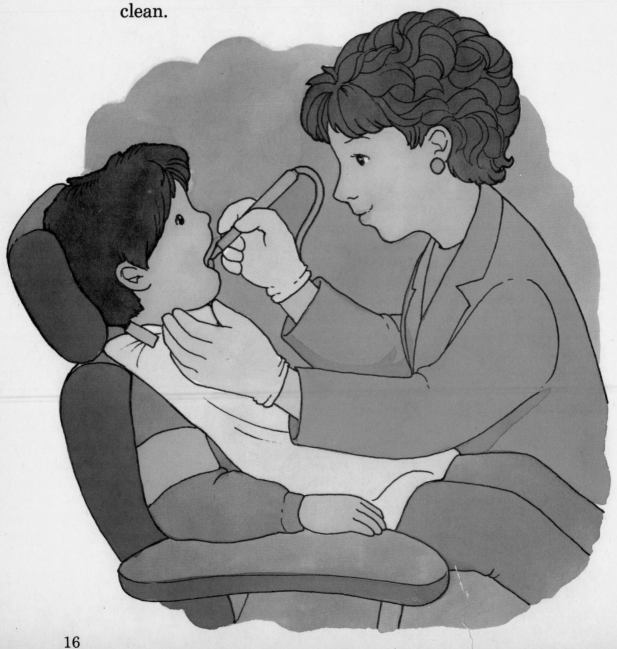

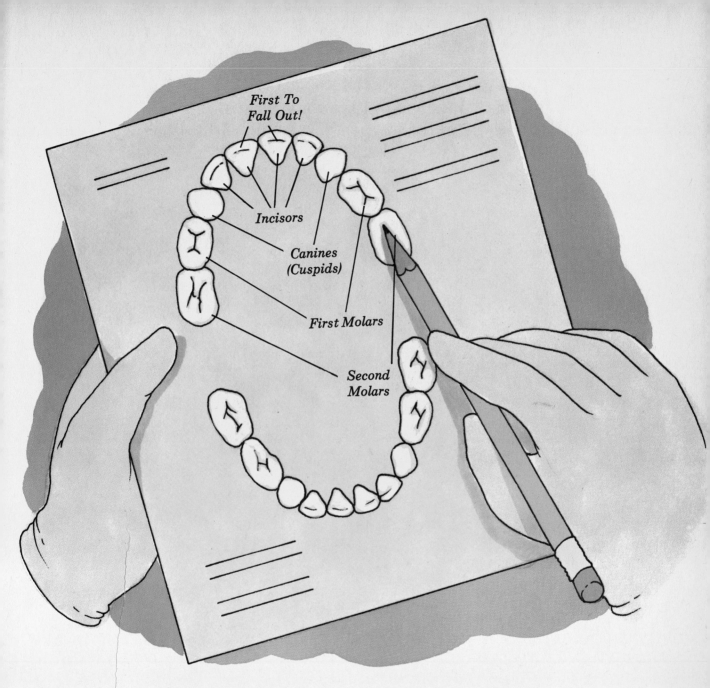

First To
Fall Out!

Incisors

Canines
(Cuspids)

First Molars

Second
Molars

Robby watches as Dr. Bennet writes on his
record card.

"This is a drawing of all the teeth in your
mouth," the dentist says. She shows it to Robby.

"I found a weak spot on *this* tooth with my explorer. I'll have to take some x rays."

Robby's eyes grow wide. He squirms in the chair.

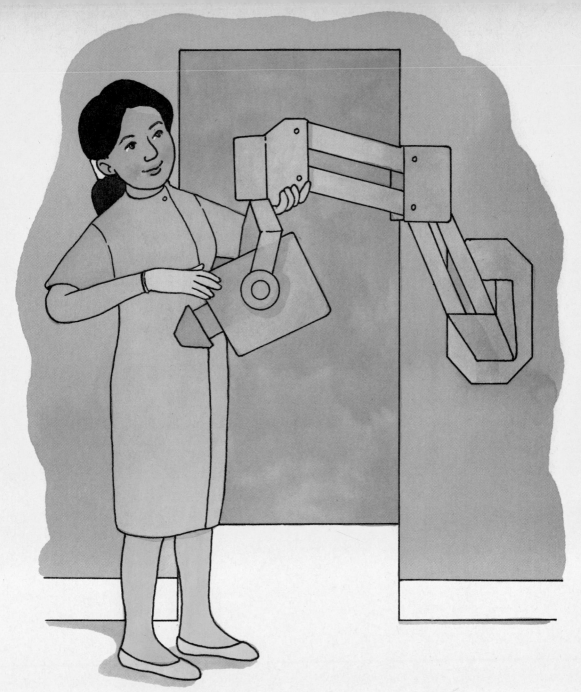

Dr. Bennet's assistant comes into the room.
She helps set up the x-ray machine.

"This machine takes very special pictures,"
Dr. Bennet says. "They show what's *inside* your
teeth!"

The assistant puts a piece of film in Robby's mouth. It is attached to a small strip of cardboard.

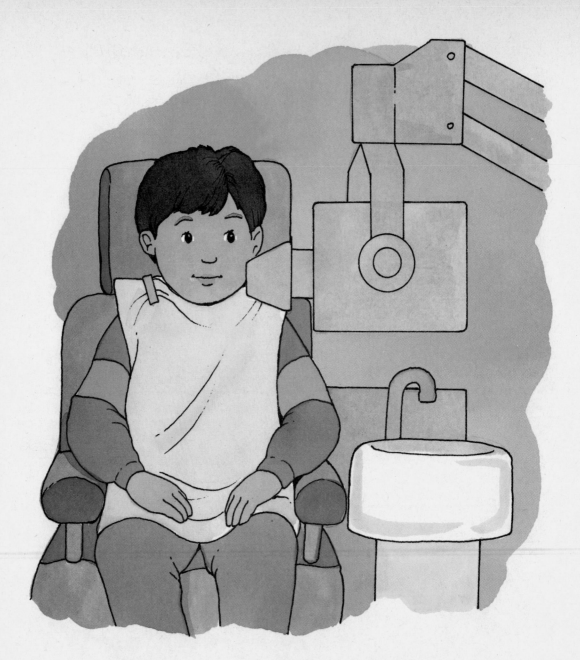

"Bite down on the cardboard," Dr. Bennet
tells Robby.

The assistant presses a button. There is a
buzzing sound as the x ray, or picture, is taken.

"All done," she says when they are through.
The assistant takes the x rays away. A short
time later, she brings them back. They have been
developed.

Dr. Bennet studies the pictures in a lighted box. She sees that Robby has a cavity, or small hole, in his weak tooth.

Dr. Bennet points out the little dark spot on the x ray of Robby's tooth.

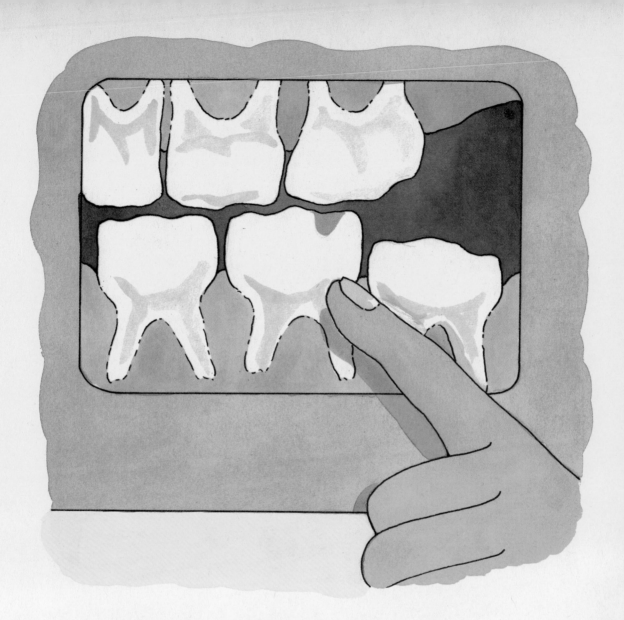

"Do you see this little cavity?" she asks
Robby. "It shows where the tooth is beginning
to decay. It's very important to clean out that
decay, before it spreads and makes the tooth too
weak to do its job. Can you come back next
week, and we'll fix that cavity?"

Robby nods.

Dr. Bennet picks up the drill once again. This time it has a special cutting tool, called a bur, on the end of it.

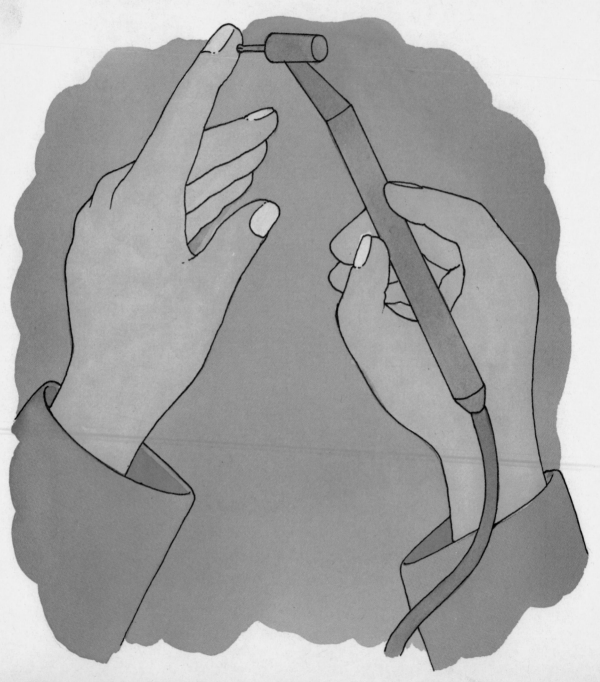

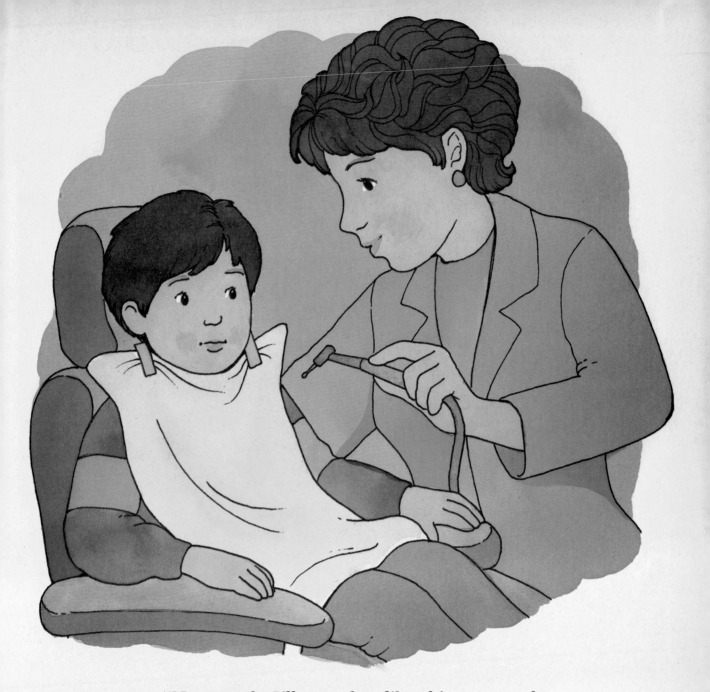

"Next week, I'll use a bur like this one to take out the decay. That will leave a tiny hole in your tooth. I'll fill the hole with silver, and your tooth will be healthy again."

Dr. Bennet shows Robby how to use a strong
thin thread, called dental floss, to clean between
his teeth. Robby laughs as he wiggles the thread
back and forth and up and down in his mouth.

"Okay, Robby. That's all for today,"
announces Dr. Bennet.
She lowers the dental chair to the floor and
takes off Robby's bib. Then she reaches into a
drawer and pulls out a brand-new toothbrush.

"This is for you, Robby," Dr. Bennet says. "Remember to brush your teeth thoroughly at least twice a day. And eat healthy foods—they're good for your teeth, too!"

Robby grins and hops out of the chair.

Dr. Bennet looks and waits.

"Robby," she finally says with a smile. "You haven't said one word yet!"

"I haven't?" Robby says. Then he laughs. "That was fun! Thanks, Dr. Bennet. See you next week."